LONDON THEN, LONDON NOW

LONDON THEN LONDON NOW

The London scene changes:
The camera does not forget

commentary by David Whitehead

London House & Maxwell
Elmsford   New York

First published 1970 by
The British Book Centre
as a London House & Maxwell book
© 1969, Dalton Watson Ltd.
Co-ordination by Richard Lawrence Associates
Printed in England by The Lavenham Press Ltd
Process Engravings by Star Illustration Works Ltd.
SBN 8277-0323-6
Library of Congress Catalog Card No. 76-116023

CONTENTS

*As it is impossible to acknowledge the source
of every photograph reproduced herewith,
the publishers are generally indebted to the
organisations listed below. Without their help
this book would not be possible.*

British Railways Board
Charrington & Company Limited
Doulton & Company Limited
Fairy Surveys Limited *(endpaper photograph)*
F. W. Woolworth & Company Limited
Greater London Council Photographic Library
Greater London Council Surveyors Department
Gamages Limited
Ind Coope Limited
John Lewis & Company Limited
J. Sainsbury Limited
London Transport Board
London Fire Brigade
Lloyds Bank Limited
Liberty's Limited
Martins Bank Limited
Marks & Spencer Limited
National Buildings Record Library
Press and Information Department, New Scotland Yard
Peter Jones (Sloane Square) Limited
Radio Times Hulton Picture Library
J. Sheekey Limited
The Courtesy of the H.M. Postmaster General
The Museum of British Transport
The Mansell Collection
The Shell-Mex and BP Group
T. Wall & Sons Limited
Truman Hanbury & Buxton Limited
Whitbread & Company Limited

INTRODUCTION

William Fox Talbot, born in 1800, shares with Daguerre the credit for first making pictures with light, and he took some of the earliest photographs in this book. Other Victorians, Edwardians, and latter-day Georgians, carry the record of old London from 1840 to 1940. By contrast, the new photographs were all taken yesterday. In pairs, the scenes from identical viewpoints tell a local story, often of change, sometimes of conservation. Together they tell a larger tale, of how changes are made, not by time but by people. London buildings do not wear out. Not age nor rot nor even total destruction in war decides whether a building remains; people choose. Through the pages there is the evidence for this. Old and new photographs of treasured buildings can look the same, even to the moss on the tiles, yet 30 years ago, between exposures, bombs left many of these churches and halls open to the weather, roofless ruins with smoke-blackened walls. The softening hand of time completes the work of the restorer, turns a forgery back into the truth. The camera does not lie, but memory can tint the picture. Was London sunnier, or were early cameras only brought out in fine weather? And memory can play false. Tram-cars are remembered with nostalgia and here may seem strangely rare, but they were never a feature of the centre, intruding only on the Embankment and through Kingsway. But if the London of the century's beginning looks smaller, that is because it was. Built to a human scale, the London of bricks and plaster was designed by individuals, for individuals. It will take time for the committees which build today to learn to do well with concrete what they have only just learned to do at all, in height and in reach. The technology of building has outstripped the art. London is choosing to destroy much of the past. London Bridge is not falling down, it is being felled. People's needs and their numbers change, and the concrete slabs reach up in response. The parks shrink and the roads swell to match the traffic. 'London Then London Now' is both an historic record, and an interim report on change.

DAVID WHITEHEAD

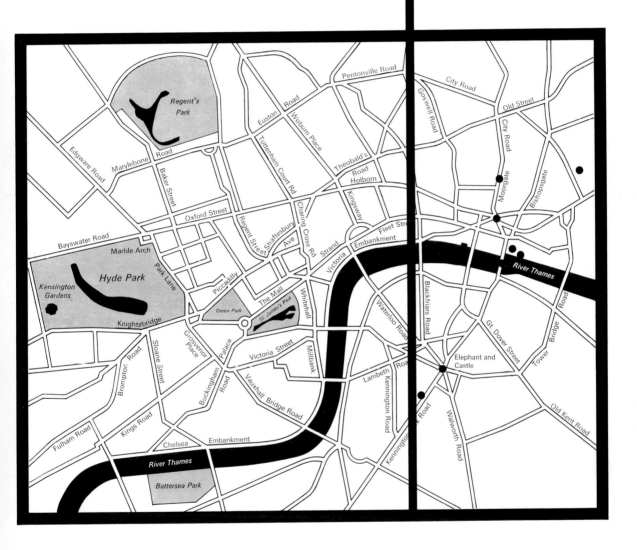

An eight mile journey west begins in the homes of London's
East End but the heart of the City is quickly reached for
all roads lead to the Bank

East End Housing

Slum clearance programmes sound drastic, once-for-all solutions to bad housing, a note of urgency heightened when the bombs of the last war smashed 24,000 homes without the formality of a demolition order. Yet re-building the East End has been going on for 100 years, from the timid tinkering of the Victorians to the £40 million rent roll of the Greater London Council today. A single neighbourhood like the Berner Estate can show changes in municipal architectural taste over 30 years. No solution is final. Even the eleven-storey flats of the Lansbury Estate in Poplar, built at the beginning of the 'sixties, with underfloor heating and soundproofing, are no longer the last word, for fashion has swung back to low-rise housing.

Billingsgate Market

The race to get the catch from the wharves on the Thames to the wholesale fish market is on at 5 a.m. every weekday morning and by a couple of hours after selling begins at six it is over. The smell lingers on, however. The central market building dates back to 1874, some 20 years before the old photograph was taken. The last-but-one porter on the right, and the porter drawing a cart on the new photograph, are wearing the traditional wood and leather hat, perhaps the same one for these are rare now and are passed on from father to son. Their flat top helps the porters bear the fish away from the market to the retailer, a hundredweight on their head at a time, a job more often done by van today.

Lower Thames Street

Billingsgate Market is in the centre of this view along Lower Thames Street from the bridge that carries King William Street across it. The buildings on the left hide change; the Old King's Head and Mermaid remains, as does Billingsgate Buildings with its stumpy tower, but the old 100 foot tower of the Coal Exchange directly behind, and everything else between here and the Tower of London (seen faintly in the background) has been cleared or rebuilt. The new tower block is

Vincula House, part of the huge development of offices and shops at Tower Place.

The Monument

It is a steep climb up the 311 steps that spiral to the top of the Monument, Sir Christopher Wren's 1677 memorial to the Great Fire of London. About its foot, one 1967 block obtrudes into the unchanged curves of earlier offices. From the top, the view is again into Lower Thames Street, showing how Billingsgate Fish Market was extended in 1961. Opposite, there is now a gap where once was the Coal Exchange but alongside, the Custom House stands where one has stood for 500 years. The present block, with some rebuilding, dates back to 1817. Down-river, Tower Bridge hides its engineering marvels (each 1,000 ton drawbridge lifting for ships in a minute and a half) behind a medieval facade. It was completed in 1894. A footway across the top is now permanently closed.

London Bridge

The press of traffic across London Bridge is nothing new. By 1905 it became so great that the width was increased by nine or ten feet and both roadway and pavements were widened. Granite pillars replaced the stone sides shown in the old photograph. Sixty years on and the decision was taken to replace Rennie's 1831 bridge. In the new photograph, London Bridge is not falling but its granite facing is being taken down stone by stone to be built again in America. On shore, new city office blocks overtop the steeples of the churches, something already begun in 1920 when the Adelaide Buildings, old home of the Pearl Assurance Company (which moved to High Holborn in 1913) was demolished in favour of the ten-storey Adelaide House. On the side of the road is the Fishmonger's Hall, built when the bridge was new.

The new tower block of Vincula House, rising above the Custom House, is the biggest change in the view downstream from London Bridge. Billingsgate Market has lost its tower but has extended sideways, and gained new wharves for neighbours. On the far right, the White Tower of the Tower of London stands on the spot it has held for nearly 900 years.

The Bank (below)

Perhaps more gold lay beneath the
Bank of England when it was long
and low than now it is seven storeys
high. The building, on the left,
was reconstructed within the old
walls (their window-spaces blind
for security) in the fifteen years
before the Second World War. Behind its freshly-cleaned facade, the
new Stock Exchange tower rises to
311 feet. Sixty-odd years earlier,
flags were at half-mast; it may be
for the death of King Edward VII,
in which event the accession of King
George V will have been proclaimed
from the steps of the Royal Exchange,
home of the Royal Exchange Insurance Companies, the third on
the site and completed in 1844. The
equestrian statue is of the Duke of
Wellington and was unveiled in his
lifetime and presence.

Finsbury Pavement

Looking towards the junction of
City Road and Tabernacle Street,
beyond the trees of Finsbury Square,
it is hard to relate the smart fronts
of today's banks and insurance
offices with those of 1911, when the
City had already extended this
far north. The candy-striped brick-
work of the upper storeys on the
right, however, identify one remnant
which has survived the trams, while
on the left, the old buildings are
intact as far as the new white shape
of Balfour House, home of the
Power-Gas Corporation.

Elephant and Castle

There was never enough room for a traffic island where the six roads met at *the Elephant*, and the trams queued for a quarter of a mile. But the early 1960's with no respect for old building lines, swept everything away, and made room. The domed underground station was the last to fall, only leaving to represent the old, the classical portico of the Metropolitan Tabernacle, burned out in the last century, bombed out in this, but rebuilt and not replaced. Behind it is the tower of the London College of Printing. Opposite is the huge shopping centre where there is no rain but plenty of wind to blow the dusty bus tickets about.

London Pubs

The whole history of London pubs is told by only two. Until the nineteenth century pubs sat low, like the earlier Red Lion, with only a room or two for the landlord above. The Victorians added more; clubrooms, and private bars and snugs, all mahogany and glass, in pubs like the earlier Prince Albert. Later came oak and tudor. It seems odd to rebuild a pub in a style earlier than that demolished, but the pseudo Tudor of between the wars was as universal as the glass and concrete of today.

The Post Office

The telegraph boy, the six postmen and their colleague below are wearing pre-1906 uniforms; the stand-up collars were winter wear and those turned down were for the summer. The men, whose wages went up to 43s. in 1912, have good conduct stripes on their chests. These were abolished in 1914. The peaked cap of the modern postman was introduced in 1932. The Post Office experimented with steam and electric motors as early as 1897 but concluded in 1902 that it had not produced a vehicle which could be 'relied upon to carry heavy loads of mails with the same regularity as vans drawn by horses'. But by 1910 it was praising the advantage to the mails of greater speed and the red mail vans grew rapidly in number after the Great War.

2

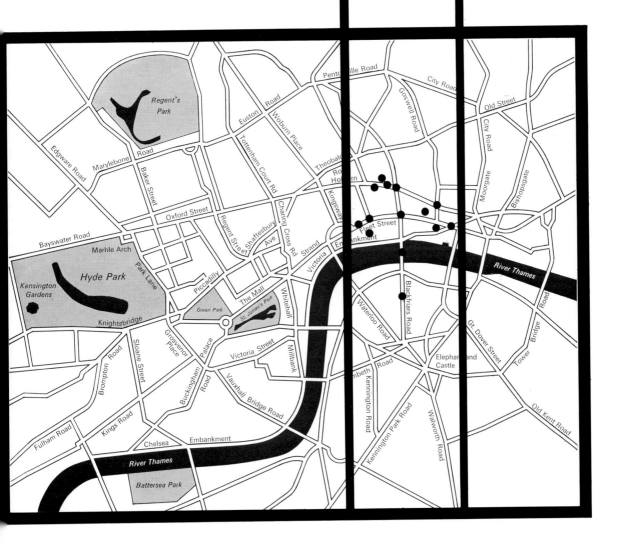

Even in scenes that do not show it, St. Paul's dominates
the City's west for the buildings curve to accommodate
its presence

Mansion House Station

Why is the Mansion House Station so far from the Mansion House? Because the Metropolitan Railway was thwarted in its bid to buy a closer site, before completing the Inner Circle in 1884. The crowded omnibus recalls the resulting preference for surface travel, for passengers would rather use the bus than walk up Queen Victoria Street to the underground station round in Cannon Street, at least until the Central Line was built to the Bank in 1900. But this scene is later, for the motor cars, with their early London and Middlesex registration marks, are squeezing out the hansom cabs and wagons. Now multiple exits from the underground station keep the bowler hats off the roadway. The sound of his bell would signal the return to the neighbourhood of the man with the grinding wheel. Blunts knives and scissors would be saved for him.

Queen Victoria Street

Considered the greatest improvement made to London in the 19th
century, Queen Victoria Street was
driven through to the City from the
Embankment, to relieve over-
crowded Cheapside. It is 100 years
old, for sections were opened between 1869 and 1871, and they
quickly became lined with commercial buildings. Few escaped the
bombing of the Second World War
unscathed. To a generation used to
the horse, the description *collecting
van for fast train traffic* on the
London and North Western Railway dray would not seem incon-
gruous; probably the van in the new
photograph makes no better time
to Euston.

Cheapside

Badly smashed by bombs, the buildings between Cheapside and St. Paul's Churchyard were replaced by a single huge structure to house additional departments of the Bank of England. It obliterates Bread Street, birthplace of Milton, although a pedestrian way, past fountains, remains. There are shops on the Cheapside frontage and, in its old position on the corner, Short's Wine Bar, with one of the old white glass lamps inside the door.

Wharves and warehouses still lie between Upper Thames Street and the river, beneath St. Paul's, but commercial sailing barges have gone. Motor-powered vessels, able to drive against the tide and work in all winds, might seem to have unbeatable advantages, but sailing barges outlasted their arrival by a surprisingly long time, carrying such loads as cement. The last, and centenary, sailing barge race in the Thames was in 1963. Large pleasure vessels may also prove a dying craft for most are elderly now, and the cost of commissioning new ones may prove inordinate. Above, a muffin man, his wares on his head.

St. Paul's Churchyard

Its buildings flattened by bombing, the junction of St. Paul's Churchyard with Cannon Street has taken a new shape. Only the tower of St. Augustine's Church survives, and has become the entrance to a low-keyed new choir school which does not compete with the mass of St. Paul's beside it. In the middleground, the old warehouses are replaced by Gateway House, the Wiggins Teape headquarters. Its south side is set back to preserve the view of the Cathedral from Cannon Street. On the right is the red-brick Bracken House, home of the Financial Times, and the offices before that are of Spillers. (Below Left: a bread van).

From St Paul's (west)

Away from the main line of Ludgate Hill and Fleet Street, the massive blocks of new buildings begin to break up the pattern imposed by the streets and it becomes hard to relate the new to the old. The churches stay as points of reference however, starting with the graceful spire of St. Martin's-within-Ludgate which the angle of view makes appear to be in the middle of Ludgate Circus. The tallest spire

n left is that of St. Bride's; once
ominant at 226 ft. but not half
ne height of the Post Office Tower,
ow on the skyline to the right.
t 550 ft. it is the tallest building
n Britain. Almost in the centre of
ne top half of the view sits the
quat tower of what seems a gothic
alace. It is the huge headquarters of
ne Prudential Assurance Company
n Holborn. In the foreground,
mmediately below the Cathedral,
is Juxon House, which has a
viewing gallery open to the public,
except in winter.

From St. Paul's (south west)

How old is the older photograph? The curves and columns of Unilever House, built on the site of De Keyser's Royal Hotel, were complete by 1934, and the Oxo warehouse across the river is a few years earlier. Is the first structure to rise above the skyline from the left a half-built Millbank Tower? False trail, a second glance confirms that it is the Chelsea gasholder, behind and not beside the triple bulk of the Imperial Chemical and Thames Houses. No trace of the Shell Centre, begun in 1957 and now dwarfing the Houses of Parliament across the river. No start made in clearing the south bank for the 1951 Festival of Britain but the clue is close; Waterloo Bridge is hardly begun, narrowing the choice to 1936 or a year either side.

Ludgate Hill

From the steps of St. Paul's, looking down Ludgate Hill, the biggest change is Juxon House, the controversial new office block of 1967. By intention, it holds back the view of the West Front of the Cathedral until those walking up the hill are in the position best to appreciate it. But the obstruction has been criticised. Sharp things were said in an earlier century about the statue of Queen Anne, for turning her back on the church. Buildings south of Ludgate Hill were least damaged by bombing, as the view on page 35 has already shown, but the survival of the cranked stackpipe above the corner, unchanged by 40 years of war and peace, is astonishing.

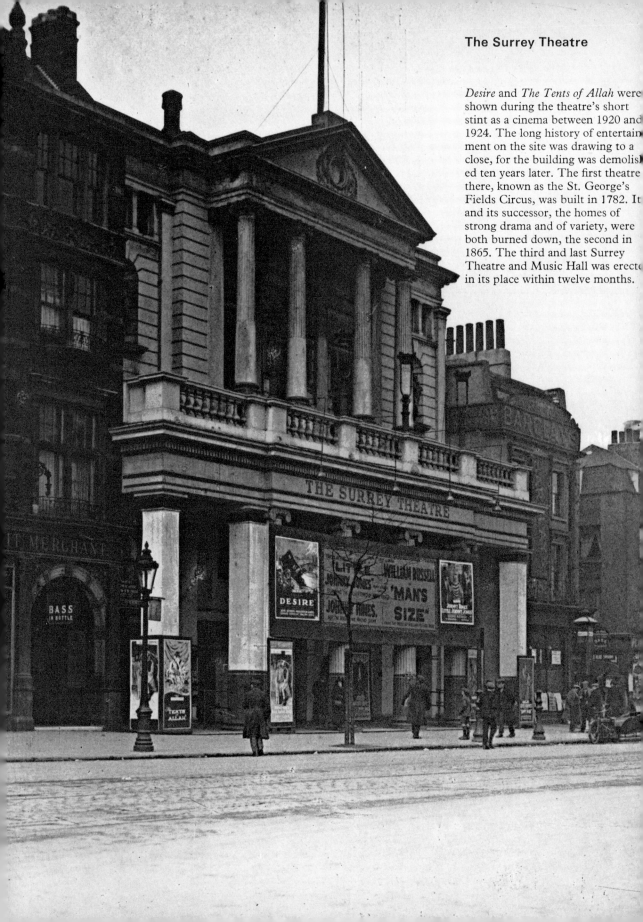

The Surrey Theatre

Desire and *The Tents of Allah* were shown during the theatre's short stint as a cinema between 1920 and 1924. The long history of entertainment on the site was drawing to a close, for the building was demolished ten years later. The first theatre there, known as the St. George's Fields Circus, was built in 1782. It and its successor, the homes of strong drama and of variety, were both burned down, the second in 1865. The third and last Surrey Theatre and Music Hall was erected in its place within twelve months.

Blackfriars Bridge

One hundred years old, the bridge
was completed at the end of 1869
and cost £350,000. After 1907, it
was widened from 80 to 100 feet
to allow the tramcars to cross and
travel along the Victoria Embankment before doubling back across
the river over Westminster Bridge.
Congestion caused by cross traffic
was tackled in 1967 when the bridge
was altered to allow Queen Victoria
Street traffic to pass under it.

Holborn Circus

From under the canopy of Gamages Store, looking towards Holborn Viaduct, nothing of the old commercial buildings remains, only the Church of St. Andrew, and beyond it, the City Temple. The Parish Church, where Thomas Chatterton, the poet, was buried, escaped the Great Fire of London but Sir Christopher Wren rebuilt it anyway, in 1686. He came back in 1704 to heighten the tower. It did not escape the bombing but was restored in 1961. The statue is of Prince Albert on horseback. The new building on the left, on the corner with Hatton Garden, was put up for the Anglo-American Corporation of South Africa in 1956. Beyond it is Atlantic House, built in 1951, a home of H. M. Stationery Office.

High Holborn

Atlantic House now fills the left of the picture, and beyond it is the gap where Farringdon Street is bridged. The viaduct and associated roadworks, begun in 1863, took nine years to complete and cost over £2 million. The City Temple, on the right, looks much the same but the old walls hide change. Opened in 1874 as a Congregational Church for 3,000 worshippers it was destroyed in 1941 and rebuilt as a 1,400 seat Church with an 800 seat theatre behind the old facade.

Gamages Store

Why is there a building of quite a different order between the matching blocks that make up the older part of Gamages? Because this was once the Bell Inn, rebuilt in 1898, which became a filling in the sandwich when the store was extended early in the century. In the older photograph, the Bell would stand to the right, for it was the western half of the new store which was built on the site of Ridler's Hotel. The eastern section did away with another hostelry, called the Black Bull.

Staple Inn (opposite page)

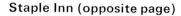

The hem-lines on the girls across the road are not much lower than those of the mini-skirts of today so the 'twenties fashion for short skirts is restored. Like the Staple Inn, and the 16th century shops at its front, which have known the restorer again and again. Yet the hand of time, which first polishes and then rubs bare is dealing kindly with the latest restorations, after a flying bomb in the Second World War compressed the ravages of centuries into seconds. In the two courts behind, the redness of new brick and tile is becoming subdued, the moss is creeping back between the cobbles, and the buildings again achieve the patina of age. In front, the stone pillar, topped by a griffin, marks the City boundary. The new slab of offices in the background is the Mirror Building.

Ludgate Circus

The bombs of the Second World War knocked some of the corners off Ludgate Circus but unchanged for nearly 300 years is the fine contrast between the dome of St. Paul's and the needle spire of St. Martin-within-Ludgate, both built by Wren at the same time. Less well regarded was the railway viaduct across Ludgate Hill. In 1863, 1,000 people petitioned the City Corporation against the disfigurement proposed but the alternatives were too costly. The new office block beyond it, built in 1962, is on the site of Messrs. Treloars' linoleum and carpet establishment. The King Lud public house, on the north east corner of the circus, looks much as it did when the earlier photograph was taken in 1913.

With the rattle of its chain drive, the thud of its solid tyres and the thump of its engine, this locomotive without rails (used to deliver fuel for the massive stationary oil engines of before the petrol era) must have been a compendium of noises.

Temple Bar

The heads of traitors and rebels were displayed on Temple Bar, the gateway between the City and Westminster, rebuilt to the design of Sir Christopher Wren after the Great Fire. Yet rooms inside it were put to a more mundane purpose; they were rented to a bank for £20 a year. Only the tower of St. Dunstan's-in-the-West, dating from 1833, links the two photographs but behind the modern newspaper offices, banks and insurance companies, old courts and houses remain. The turning on the right, beneath the arch, leads into the Temple.

Royal Courts of Justice

The entrance giving on to the Strand from the Law Courts is for admission to the public galleries, from where justice may be seen freely dispensed between 10 a.m. and 4.15 p.m. when the courts are sitting. So long did the building of this Gothic pile take that its architect, G. E. Street, who began it in 1874, after years of procrastination over the site, did not live to see its completion. His son, A. E. Street, inherited the task, and finished it eight years later, with the help of Sir Arthur Blomfield. To mark where the Strand and Westminster end, and Fleet Street and the City begin, the griffin on his pedestal stands in front of where the triple-arched Temple Gate stood, as its memorial. The man in the bowler hat is selling Sherbet Water at 1d. or ½d. a glass and the griffin on the lamp post shows that he is on the City side.

Middle Temple

Sanctuary from the traffic of Fleet Street in the peace of Middle Temple, the home of lawyers and their students for 600 years. In Fountain Court, looking up the steps into New Court, there are fewer flowers than when Dickens imagined the meetings between Ruth Pinch and her brother Tom in Martin Chuzzlewit. Gravel and paving are easier to tend and there is still strong colour, from the leaves and from the goldfish in the pool.

NEW COURT MIDDLE TEMPLE B-837.

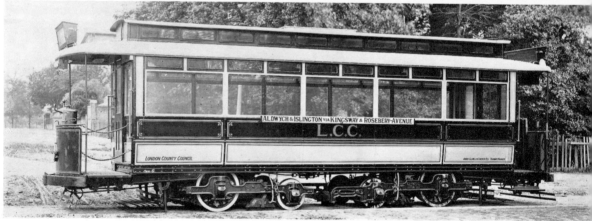

Transport

What could be more English than the *London General Omnibus Company*? Yet, oddly, this was no other than the *French General Omnibus Company of London*, given a new name and a local management after it had taken over a group of small operators in 1856. The first horse-drawn omnibuses with stairs to the upper-deck were introduced in about 1864. Earlier, access to the roof was by a set of iron rungs up the side, a climb no lady undertook. Horse-buses lingered until 1910, after motor-buses had been introduced in 1904, the year that the Kingsway tram tunnel was under construction. The tram-car is of that period, for the route was first opened as far as the Aldwych, and was extended to the Embankment in 1907. Single-decked trams lasted until 1930, when the tunnel was deepened to allow the passage of the double-decked trams used on the rest of the system. The last ran in 1952, but the influence of trams on the public transport system remains, for many red London Routemaster buses follow the old tram routes as closely as if still guided by the rails.

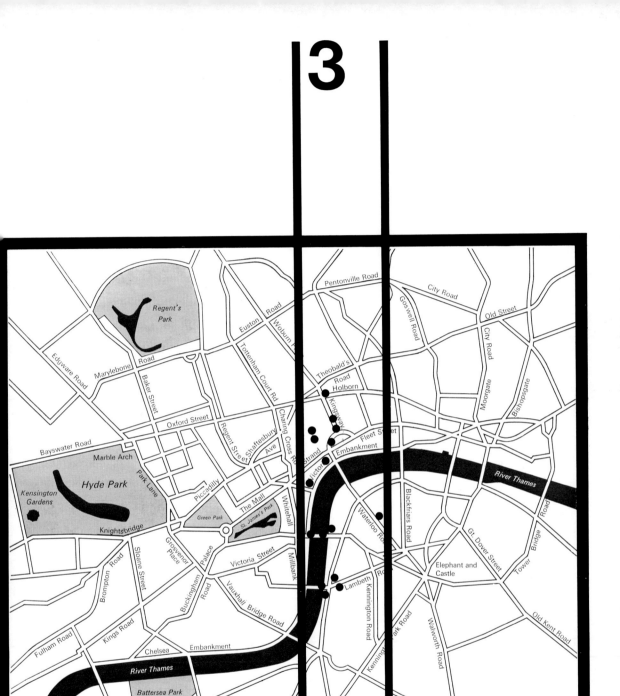

Celebrating London's local government, the camera passes
from its great twentieth century road and bridge works to
its riverbank home in Lambeth

The Aldwych

Those noble columns on the Gaiety Theatre were not included in the original plans for it but London County Council offered to pay for them in order to dignify the new Aldwych development. When the bill was presented, however, the LCC disputed the amount and only paid after losing a court case. The new Gaiety Theatre was built in 1903 to replace the old, which was in the way of the Aldwych road-works. George Edwardes had made the old theatre the home of musical comedy, and the tradition was continued in the new, after his death, with productions like *Our Miss Gibbs* and *Tonight's the Night* (with Leslie Henson). The theatre closed with *Running Wild* in 1939 when it was managed by Firth Shepherd, Richard Hearne and Fred Emney. It was demolished, and the English Electric headquarters put up in 1960. When the earlier photograph was taken, the Waldorf Hotel, opened in 1906, was under construction.

Newest of the great London thoroughfares, Kingsway was laid out as an act of faith by the London County Council between 1900 and 1905. Sites alongside it were slow to let at first and it was not until 1922, three years before the earlier photograph was taken, that the last building was erected. In 1929 the pickaxes were back, for the tram tunnel linking Kingsway with the Victoria Embankment was deepened to allow double-decked tramcars to use it. These ran until 1952 when the tunnel was closed. Eleven years later it was turned into an underpass for northbound motor cars.

The Stoll

The London Opera House was
built by Oscar Hammerstein of
New York in 1910 at a cost of
£200,000 but it flopped and Sir
Oswald Stoll turned it into a cinema.
Later, musical comedy was presented there by Prince Littler. In
the office block built in its stead
entertainment retains a stake for the
Royalty cinema is tucked away
behind and below. The block is the
headquarters of the Guest Keen and
Nettlefold group of companies and
part of it served for a time as the
first offices of the British Steel
Corporation.

High Holborn

Easy to date the older photograph for the huge headquarters of the Pearl Assurance Company, with its lofty clocktower, was under construction in 1912. It sprouted wings in the thirties and again in the sixties, all to a new building line that is not followed by the rest of the blocks of offices and shops between it and the junction with Kingsway. The road was never widened, but is now one-way at this end.

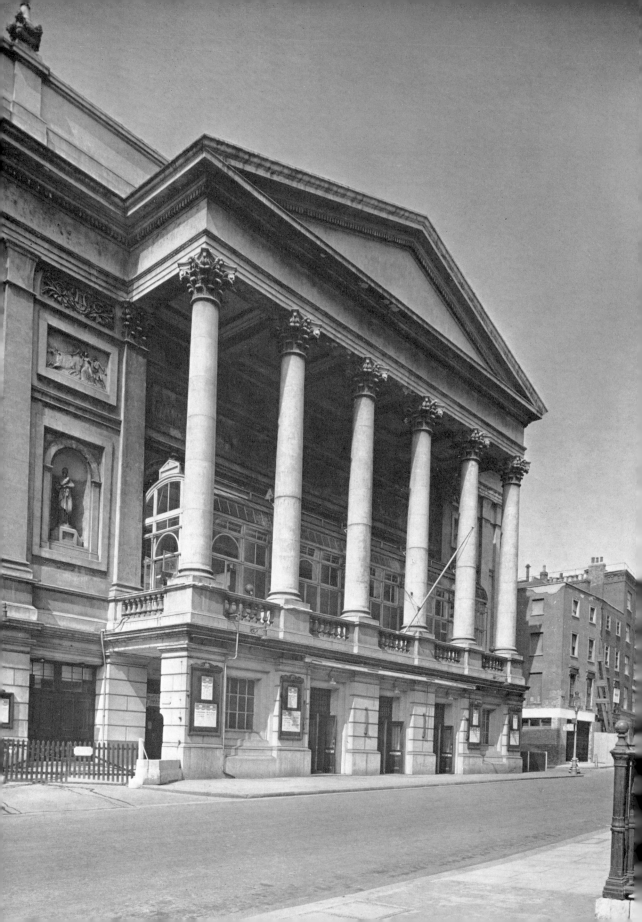

Royal Opera House, Covent Garden

When the first theatre, in the likeness of a Grecian temple, was built in 1808 the customers rioted for 61 nights at the increased prices made necessary by the £150,000 expended. Women wore medals inscribed OP for old prices, and men wore the same letters in their hats. Eventually the management had to give way, but the publicity attracted by the riots meant they were not the losers; the theatre was packed. It was burned down in 1856 and rebuilt: the statues on the front, by Flaxman, were saved from the old building. Although the sumptuous home of opera and ballet for a hundred years, and the British equivalent of the great state opera houses on the Continent, the Covent Garden theatre has, on occasion, compromised its dignity with cinema shows, revues, and even a prize-fight.

Coopes & Humphreys Ltd 71 Newman St

Vans and lorries have replaced
wagons, and the round wicker baskets
that the porters would stack on
their heads are fewer, but the fruit,
flowers and vegetables of the wholesale market still spill across the

pavements from the early hours of
the morning. Long threatened with
a move to ease the congestion, the
market seems certain to find a new
home at Nine Elms, Vauxhall, and
the link with the fruitful earth will
be broken for Covent is a contrac-
tion of Convent, and this was the
garden of the monks of Westminster
Abbey. The St. Paul's Church sign
in the new photograph does not
label the central market building
put up in 1831-33 but points to
the Parish Church in the north west
corner, designed by Inigo Jones
who first laid out the square.

The Playhouse

Neither the affection felt for Miss
Gladys Cooper, nor the outside of
the Playhouse changed much in the
years between the photographs,
but entry has become cheaper. A
seat in the gallery used to cost 1s.,
now it is free, for the BBC has the
theatre for broadcasting and tickets
for many shows are
given away on

application. The Playhouse was
known as the Avenue Theatre before
it had to be completely rebuilt in
1905 after part of the roof of Charing
Cross Station had fallen into it,
causing tremendous damage.

The Old Vic

Opened as the Coburg, with a
production of *Trial by Battle*, or
Heaven Defend the Right in 1818,
the theatre in Waterloo Bridge Road
was renamed the Victoria after a
visit from the Princess and future
Queen. It became a music hall and
was failing when the first woman
member of the LCC, the formidable
Emma Cons, bought it and re-
opened it as "The Royal Victoria
Hall and Coffee Tavern", on Boxing
Day 1880, but the "Old Vic" title
was already established, and stuck.
It became the home of Shakespeare
after 1914 but the bombs of the
next world war left the Old Vic
Company homeless. The building
was repaired, and flourishes, while
the new National Theatre Company
waits for its new home on the South
Bank.

The River

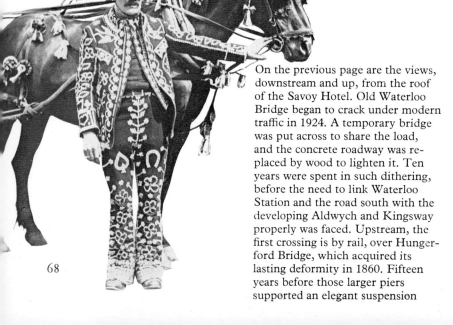

On the previous page are the views, downstream and up, from the roof of the Savoy Hotel. Old Waterloo Bridge began to crack under modern traffic in 1924. A temporary bridge was put across to share the load, and the concrete roadway was replaced by wood to lighten it. Ten years were spent in such dithering, before the need to link Waterloo Station and the road south with the developing Aldwych and Kingsway properly was faced. Upstream, the first crossing is by rail, over Hungerford Bridge, which acquired its lasting deformity in 1860. Fifteen years before those larger piers supported an elegant suspension bridge. The coming of the railway to Charing Cross ended its short life on the Thames, and steel girders were laid across its stumps, but it was re-erected across the Clifton Gorge at Bristol and remains there today. Beyond the *char*, or bend in the river, are Westminster and Lambeth bridges. The sailing barges stand off the wharves where County Hall now stands and when workmen dug into the banks to lay the foundation in 1910 they uncovered an earlier vessel, a Roman Galley of oak, 50 foot long. The headquarters of the present Greater London Council, successors to the old LCC, grew slowly. Electorial reverse by those who supported the construction enabled those who thought it an extravagance to delay buying Holloway's wharf (directly above) and leave off the east wing. The resulting building had a lop-sided look at the opening in 1922 but the missing wing was added later and more wings built behind. In the splendour of sequins is a pearly king.

The River (continued)

Both Europe's *most magnificent hotel* and its *finest bridge* have been abstracted from this view down river. On the left, the Hotel Cecil, built in 1896, was demolished in 1930 to make way for Shell Mex House (which has the largest clock in London). John Rennie's Waterloo Bridge, completed in 1817, was replaced by the present structure just before the Second World War (although not officially opened until after it). Behind it runs the long line of Somerset House. Beside the Hotel Cecil stands the Savoy Hotel, the older by seven years. The terraced balconies to each floor were removed in 1912. Cleopatra's Needle is 68½-ft. tall and once stood outside the Temple of Heliopolis in Egypt. It has a twin in Central Park, New York. The sea passage of the obelisk between 1877-78 took so long because the first vessel carrying it was wrecked off the coast of Spain. Pleasure vessels have plied on the Thames since 1815 when a Mr. George Dodd fitted out a steamship for this purpose.

Building the County Hall took half a century, for it was not until 1963 that the south block, on the right of the new photograph, was completed. Already a start must have been made in bringing London's local government across the Thames when the old photograph was taken or half of New Scotland Yard (see entire on the opposite bank) was not completed until 1912, the year the foundation stone of the County Hall was laid. Work on the foundations had begun in 1909, and the building was opened in 1922. Except in times of war, building and planning extensions and improvements has been continuous ever since; first a wing left off for economy, finished in 1933, then a central portion of an extension behind, finished in 1939, then an arm to the north, finished in 1958, and then the southerly block. As well as the council chamber and ceremonial offices, the three buildings that now comprise the County Hall house 7,000 people.

Lambeth Bridge

Tagged the cheapest and ugliest bridge ever built, old Lambeth suspension bridge was put up by a private company in 1862 for £40,000 and that included the land. It looks deserted because for years before its demolition in 1929 it was closed to all but pedestrians. Within four years the scene was as it is today, a new bridge with Horseferry Road skirted by ICI House, and its companion, Thames House, with their 500 foot of frontage to the river between them. ICI House replaced an old brewery behind which can just be detected the campanile of Westminster Cathedral.

The Albert Embankment

Not all trace of the magnificent terra-cotta palace that once housed the Doulton pottery works has vanished, for a fragment remains as a red glow hidden behind the 1937 headquarters of the London Fire Brigade on the right of the new photograph. On the other side of the former W H Smith building, which carries 'to let' signs, is Doulton's new office block. Not a riot of applied decoration to compare with its predecessor, it is brightened by a few of the company's tiles, chiefly in gold.

Lambeth High Street

Decay had bitten deeply into Old Lambeth when the Onward Working Men's Club leaned on wooden crutches in the last century. Now the High Street shrinks behind the tall office blocks that front on to the Albert Embankment. The bill beneath the barber's window, for Madame Tussaud's waxworks, advertises *The Court with W. E. Gladstone*, the Liberal Prime Minister. He died in 1898, four years after last holding office. The posters on the left announce events at the Crystal Palace which was moved from Hyde Park to Sydenham in 1854. It was burned down in 1936, a year after this office block was built for W. H. Smith, the booksellers. It has a prominent clock on the front. Smith's moved their wholesaling department out to Swindon in 1967, after which the block stood empty. In the background is a corner of the Decca building.

Lambeth Palace

For seven centuries, the London home of the Archbishops of Canter bury, Lambeth Palace looks un changed, but the gatehouse called Morton's Tower (after the Cardinal who built it in 1490) and the 15th century tower of St. Mary's Parish Church are exceptional. Most of the palace is later than its gate and all of the church is later than its tower, and both needed careful restoration after a wartime battering from bombs badly aimed at the Houses of Parliament across the river. The distant tower on the left of the new photograph is the Shell building.

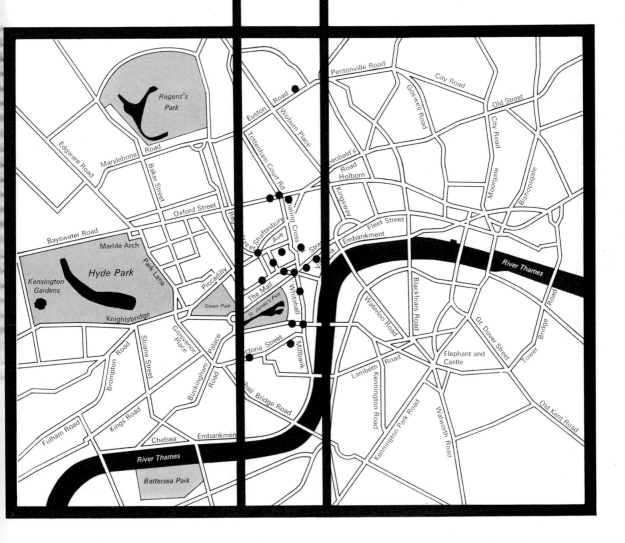

The West End, where theatres and music halls may give
way to cinemas and slot machines but the fascination for
the sightseer does not change

The Strand

The old 'Tiv' had a short, but a gay life. Built on the site of a beer hall in 1890, the music hall where Lottie Collins sang *Ta-Ra-Ra-Boom-De-Ay* was pulled down for road widening in 1914 and the plan to reconstruct it was halted by the Great War. The ground became a recruiting centre for Lord Kitchener's army, and the Canadian YMCA had a hut on it. The Tivoli Picture Theatre was built in 1922 but was bombed in the Second World War. The Peter Robinson store rose in its stead. Post-war Strand ends with Villiers House, on the corner of Villiers Street (overleaf), after which little has changed since the last century. The Charing Cross Hotel was built in 1864. It was the first of the big London hotels. In the same year a replica of the Eleanor Cross, last of the nine crosses put up by Edward I, to mark the progress towards her funeral in Westminster Abbey of his dear and affectionate wife, was erected in the forecourt, near the site of the original. The street looks busier and more spirited in the old than the new, perhaps because travellers were not closed away inside their conveyances but rode on top, in front, and behind them.

St. Martin's Court

The astounding rise in the fortunes
of the oyster, is reflected in the
changes to Sheekey's Oyster Bar and
Fish Restaurant, tucked away
between the theatres of the Charing
Cross Road and St. Martin's Lane.
Although the facade remains, the
open-fronted shop of old, ready to
dispense oysters by the barrelful,
has given way to the enclosed
restaurant of today, where oysters
may be savoured by the half-dozen.
Ice-cream, by contrast, has
taken an opposite course. Once only
to be obtained from Italian crafts-
men, equipped to produce and preserve it, this former specialism may
be picked out of any deep-freeze.

Trafalgar Square

Nearly 40 years after he fell in the Battle of Trafalgar, Nelson's statue was put upon its column to stand 176 feet high, or 16 feet lower than the Monument. This was in 1843 and with the exception of Landseer's lions, which were not delivered for another 25 years (although often promised earlier) it completed the national memorial to England's greatest naval hero. The National Gallery was built at the same time as the square was laid out, using the portico and columns from Carlton House, the mansion which stood at the foot of Regent Street until the Regent, George IV, tired of it. So was the Unionist Club, on the west side. Early a centre for those who agitated for change, the square is little changed itself. The Unionist Club was fashioned into Canada House in 1925, and the Government of South Africa bought Morley's Hotel, and built South Africa House in its place in 1931-33.

The Church of St. Martin is a hundred years older than any neighbouring building. Its architect was James Gibbs, a follower of Sir Christopher Wren. Behind it, in St. Martin's Lane, is the dome of the Coliseum. Widely different entertainment has been offered there in this century. Built as a music hall, it was more successful as a theatre (*White Horse Inn* ran for 651 performances) and it introduced wide-screen cinema. Now it is the home of the Sadler's Wells opera company. The statue of Charles I in the foreground by Hubert Le Seur was cast in 1633, but the Civil War broke out before it could be erected. It was sold as scrap to a John Rivet who produced souvenirs, allegedly made from it, yet was able to produce it entire at the Restoration. In the pavement behind it, a bronze plaque marks the official centre of London, from which measurements of mileage are taken. The road-sweeper is propelled by horse-power but has an interesting mechanical drive.

87

Of the two older photographs,
the smaller is the earlier because,
edging in on the right, are the
buildings that the War Office,
Portland stonework shining, re-
places on the larger picture. It must
have been brand new then, for the
missing statue of the Duke of Cambridge was cast also in 1899, and
within two years it was joined by the
block now shared by the Crown
Estates Office and the Ministry of
Agriculture, Fisheries and Food,
on its far side. On its near side, is
Inigo Jones's great banqueting hall,
all that left his drawing board of a
great new palace planned for King
James I, and all that remains of the
Tudor palace to which it was added.
The Royal United Services Institu-
tion is next door, on the far right
of the long photograph. On the left
is the old Admiralty and down the
centre, Earl Haig has ridden ahead of
the Duke of Cambridge since 1936.

Cockspur Street

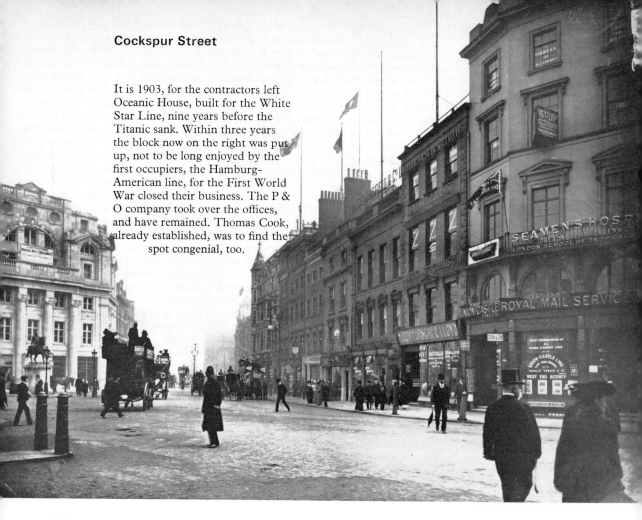

It is 1903, for the contractors left Oceanic House, built for the White Star Line, nine years before the Titanic sank. Within three years the block now on the right was put up, not to be long enjoyed by the first occupiers, the Hamburg-American line, for the First World War closed their business. The P & O company took over the offices, and have remained. Thomas Cook, already established, was to find the spot congenial, too.

Cranbourn Street

Entertainment is still the business of Cranbourn Street, between Leicester Square and Charing Cross Road. Daly's Theatre was built by George Edwardes for the American manager, Augustin Daly, and became the second home of musical comedy, after the Gaiety. In the 44 years before it was demolished to make way for the cinema in 1937, its biggest success was *The Maid of The Mountains* which ran for 1,352 performances in the Great War. To the left, the twin buildings of the Hotel and Cafe de Europe, and the Queen's Hotel, standing each side of Leicester Place, are hotels no longer but offices above eating places. Beyond them is the Empire Palace of Varieties, which has become the Empire Cinema. The caryatides above the Slot Palace are on the combined Cranbourn Mansions and Hippodrome Theatre building where live entertainment continues in "The Talk of the Town".

Leicester Square (Odeon)

The bills on the front of the old Alhambra say *Gracie Fields* but they might be advertising one of the Lancashire Lass's films, and not a personal appearance, for the building served as a cinema from 1929 until it was demolished in 1936. First opened as the Panopticum of Science and Art in 1854 it was intended to be a place of popular instruction, like the Polytechnic, but the venture failed. Re-opened as a theatre and music hall in 1871 it had a run of more than half a century. Perhaps its best remembered success was *The Bing Boys are Here* with George Robey in 1916. The Odeon, built in its stead, has acquired some age of its own now but time has not mellowed the forbidding black exterior, which belies the exceptional comfort inside. It has recently been refurbished.

Leicester Square (continued)

The trees in the square were planted in 1874 so the camera catches them early and late in a century of growth. The old Empire Theatre was opened in 1883; sometimes presenting straight plays and sometimes variety. Its promenade was attacked as a haunt of vice by Mrs. Ormiston Chant in her purity campaign of 1894. The publicity increased profits. The theatre was demolished in 1927 and a cinema built. To the left is Stagg and Mantle, one of the earliest big clothiers in London, established in 1812. The hotel and Cafe de Europe, rebuilt in 1898 as the Queen's Hotel, is now offices hiding above the hoardings and eating houses of today. The statue of Shakespeare is as old as the trees and was copied from the memorial in Westminster Abbey. Behind it is the Dental Hospital, rebuilt in 1906 on the other side of St. Martin Street. On its old site is the Leicester Square Theatre, recently reconstructed.

The Automobile Association

Founded in 1905, the AA moved into the headquarters shown in Whitcomb Street, backing onto Leicester Square, in 1909 and gradually expanded to take over the west side of the square. Its first patrolman, Arthur Drew, on his cycle, warned members of police speed traps on the Brighton Road by failing to offer a salute. The road patrols were equipped with motorcycles (that shown is of 1913) but these have given way to mini-cars. More changes lie in the future. The Fanum House headquarters may be given up and a new uniform has been designed.

Haymarket (looking north)

The Carlton Hotel, on the left, was blitzed, leaving Her Majesty's Theatre a bereaved twin, for both were built to look like one at the end of the last century. An earlier Her Majesty's with a famous colonnade had stood on the same corner site. It made way for the hotel, moving up the road. To the new theatre, the last of the great actor managers, Sir Herbert Beerbohm Tree, crossed from the Theatre Royal. Now the truncated New Zealand House has the corner, its lopped look the result of planners' pruning. Barclay's Bank, in Kinnaird House, was rebuilt in stone instead of Georgian brick and stucco, to match the grandeur of the Carlton, and survives it.

Haymarket (looking south)

No motor-cabs share the ranks with hansoms but the century is this, for Dewar House was built for the whisky distillers in 1906. The Theatre Royal looks as it is since 1821, for whatever changes are made inside, sentiment preserves the Nash portico. Here, a Henry Fielding slur shocked the Prime Minister into setting the Lord Chamberlain at censoring plays, a power only recently ended. Flags still fly about the P & O shipping office in Cockspur Street, but the lantern is lost.

Piccadilly Circus

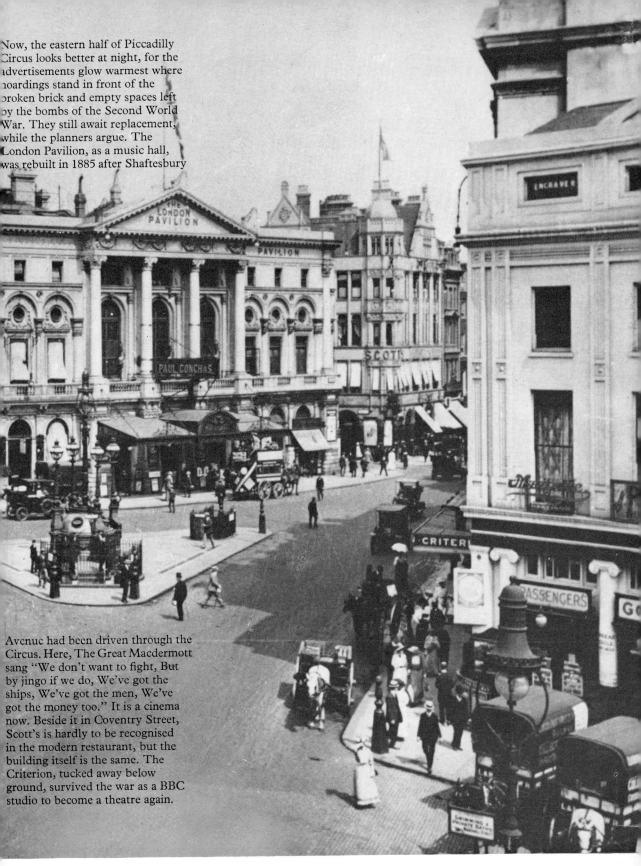

Now, the eastern half of Piccadilly Circus looks better at night, for the advertisements glow warmest where hoardings stand in front of the broken brick and empty spaces left by the bombs of the Second World War. They still await replacement, while the planners argue. The London Pavilion, as a music hall, was rebuilt in 1885 after Shaftesbury

Avenue had been driven through the Circus. Here, The Great Macdermott sang "We don't want to fight, But by jingo if we do, We've got the ships, We've got the men, We've got the money too." It is a cinema now. Beside it in Coventry Street, Scott's is hardly to be recognised in the modern restaurant, but the building itself is the same. The Criterion, tucked away below ground, survived the war as a BBC studio to become a theatre again.

Piccadilly Circus (continued)

The Royal architect Nash carried Regent Street across Piccadilly so as to avoid St. James's Church, and built the Quadrant to correct its course towards Regent's Park. His scheme was completed by 1820. The crossing was called the first Regent Circus and kept that name, and roughly this appearance, for the rest of the 19th century. The years of change began in 1907 with the building of the Piccadilly Hotel, with frontages both on to Piccadilly, and Regent Street, behind the Swan and Edgar store. Over the next 20 years, Regent Street, its Quadrant and the circus buildings were rebuilt.

Piccadilly Circus (east)

Piccadilly Circus is no longer a circus, because the buildings about it are not curved (not even the traffic goes round it) and the statue at its centre is not of Eros, the Greek God of Love. The winged archer represents the Angel of Christian Charity, for it is on a monument to the seventh Earl of Shaftesbury, who was a philanthropist, not a philanderer. Nobody cares for such fine points of detail, but everybody cared, however, when Eros was removed to the Embankment Gardens for the building of the largest underground station in London, beneath the circus. Hard to imagine Piccadilly Circus without Eros, yet in 1928, the year the station was finished, and the year the Noel Coward play *This Year of Grace* was running at the London Pavilion, there was no winged archer. Public outcry forced its return.

Pall Mall

The great clubs preserve their
anonymity. No name-plates tell
the curious that, from the right of
the new photograph, it is the Reform, the Travellers and the side
of the Athenaeum that stretch back
to Waterloo Place. The old photograph shows the Reform's old
neighbour, the Carlton, perhaps
the grandest of these palaces, but
the building was destroyed by
bombing and is replaced by a bank.
On the north side, New Zealand
House now peers from the site of
the other lost Carlton, the hotel
once on the corner with the Hay-
market. But the old photograph is
earlier than that, for the site was
occupied until 1895 by Her Majesty's
Theatre, and its famous colonnade
shows up in the distance.

Metropolitan Police

New Scotland Yard on the Victoria
Embankment was the home of the
Metropolitan Police until 1967 but
the familiar linked blocks were not
built together. Part was erected in
1891 and part in 1912. A half century on and the police moved to a
new office block in Broadway. Today, policemen on their beat are
in touch with their stations by pocket
radio but in 1920, when collapsible
aerials were fitted to the Crossley
lorry for use by the Flying Squad,
such miniaturization was not imagined. Three-wheelers for carting

away those drunk and incapable of caring for themselves, leave the occupant little dignity, but Black Marias, with their sightless windows, still deserve awe. If you ask directions of a New York policeman he is liable to rap out "Buy a map", but not the London bobby. Women police were first enrolled in the last two years of the World War I. There are more than 500 in London today. The organisation of the river police is older than that of the Metropolitan Police, of which they now form the Thames Division. Steam launches replaced rowing boats in 1885, motor-boats were introduced in 1912 and fast diesel launches became universal after 1940.

Parliament Square
(from Great George Street)

This is 1898, the year clearance began of all the buildings between Parliament Street and St. James's Park. Preparation of the huge site alone took two years and building the new government offices took another fifteen. From the 320-ft. clock tower of the Houses of Parliament, Big Ben had already been tolling the hours for 40 years. The buildings furthest away are of St. Thomas's Hospital, across the river. Perhaps the outline is familiar, while the position is odd, for the hospital was built in seven identical blocks with those up-river surviving longest. Those shown were battered out of recognition by German bombs a quarter century before replacement of the rest began.

The government offices put up in the first seven years of the century on the corner of Parliament Street and Great George Street, seem to fill the site left by the old buildings neatly but the appearance is deceptive. Parliament Street was almost trebled in width in the improvement, so that the new is far to the left of the old. It obliterates King Street, once the main road into Whitehall. Along it, King Charles I rode to trial, and Cromwell lived there at the time of the Royal Execution. Its old termination in Parliament Square can be seen beside the Luncheon and Dining Rooms.

Dean's Yard

Beside the Abbey is Dean's Yard,
providing the great Westminster
public school with its playing field.
On the north side, a row of eight
houses was designed with a style in
keeping with the Abbey by Sir
Giles Gilbert Scott and erected in
1854. These are commercial offices
now, and when they fell out of
private use and an extension at the
back was required, care was taken
to keep this, too, in the gothic style.
However a stone more porous than
that used to build the houses has
taken up more London soot so that
the extension looks older than the
houses, older than the Abbey even,
where this has been cleaned!

Victoria Street

The frontages on the left crumbled into history more suddenly than the demolition men had intended. They collapsed into the road overnight, but nobody was hurt. They look old, but their replacement by the glass and concrete Mobile House is such a short time ago that the youngest reader may remember them, and start nostalgia here. Apartments which lined both sides of the street were once ahead of their time for they were among the first to have hot-water heating instead of coal fires. Those on the right gave way to the Army and Navy Stores, whose present frontage dates from 1924. Big changes are planned for it. Opposite, The Albert public house remains, making a virtue of its 19th century look. The late Victorian office block, beyond it, has what may be the largest sash windows ever made, on its further side. The decoration on the front is larger than life, too. In 1861, an

American, a Mr. Train, laid tram-car rails on top of Victoria Street but the carriages found them such a nuisance that he was required to remove them in the same year. Recessed tram rails came later and reduced the rattle of, amongst other things, milk-carts.

SCHWEPPES
SODA WATER
GINGER ALE
WHISKY
CIGARETTES
HOMPSON
CHESS
SMOKING SALOON
HAIR CUTTING
4D.
SHAVING 2D
THE TOTTENHAM
TOILET SALOON
SHAVING 2D
AFTERNOON TEA
TEA ROOM
TROUSERS 7/6
TAILORS
Tea Rooms J.P. Restaurants Ltd Tea Rooms
TEAS
WILLESDEN (8) OLD FORD
DEWAR'S "WHITE LABEL"
SHEPHERD'S BUSH
"WHITE LABEL"
UNDERGROUND
CONTINUOUS SERVICE OF TRAINS TO
CHARING CROSS EUSTON CAMDEN TOWN
CHALK FARM HAMPSTEAD GOLDERS GREEN
TOWN HIGHGATE ETC
BLOGG'S BREWERY LTD.
SWAN VESTAS
VICTORI

St. Giles Circus (south)

Like the sweet smell which once hung about this end of Charing Cross Road, traces of the old Crosse and Blackwell jam and pickle factory linger on. The tower of seaside rock has a coat of stucco now but it ends at the spire, where the alternate bands of brick and stone still show. They show too, on the side of the Astoria, suggesting that this 1927 cinema owes more than its site to C&B, in spite of its changed roofline and round tower. The pickle factory may have become a cinema and the tea shop a bank, but all the buildings from here to Oxford Street are the same as when haircutting cost 4d. and trousers from Thompsons the tailor were 7s. 6d. Only the shop fronts have been rebuilt. In contrast, the opposite side of the road is unrecognizable. All the old buildings have gone and, inside the courtyard, out of sight, the 33 storeys of Centre Point tower over the corner. Advertisements are not so numerous as when every bus seat said Pears Soap. Compare route numbers. The same No. 24 bus travels the same road to Victoria, insofar as one-way traffic allows.

St. Giles Circus (north)

The Horseshoe Hotel, just recognizable on the right, had a brewery for a neighbour until the Dominion Cinema, perennial home of long-running musicals, began shouldering up to it in 1929. Once those horses and carriages were replaced by motor-vehicles, this end of Tottenham Court Road was to prove one of the most notorious traffic bottlenecks in London, until the buildings on the left were cleared and the new ones set well back. In the distance, the massive bulk of the Euston Centre now rises.

The New Oxford Theatre was the old Oxford music hall, one of the earliest and most popular of the palaces of variety. George Robey and Harry Tate made their debuts there. Often burned out, the Oxford was last rebuilt in 1892 and became a theatre when variety faded. The J. Lyons company, whose white and gold teashop next-door-but-one is not much altered, built the restaurant now, The Blue Diamond amusement arcade, in 1926-28, maintaining a tradition of eating and entertainment. Earlier it was the site of the Boar and Castle Inn, a hostelry dating back to Jacobean times.

St. Giles-in-the-Fields

The fine baroque spire of the church
of St. Giles soars to 160 ft. but
now the 33 storeys of Centre Point,
the office block set where
Charing Cross Road meets New
Oxford Street, go on up for twice
that height. There has been a church
here for 850 years although the
present building dates from 1733,
and its interior was restored in 1953.
Centre Point was completed in 1965.

St Pancras Station (overleaf)

To its admirers a palace that restores romance to travel, to its detractors a wildly inappropriate Victorian extravagance, this London terminus inspires more affection or distaste than most. Built for half a millions pounds as the 600 bed Grand Midland Hotel, Sir George Gilbert Scott's masterpiece opened in 1874, and became offices in 1935. Although the hotel reached back into French and Italian architectural history, the train vault behind owed nothing to past styles. Its size, and its 240 foot of unsupported span were unprecedented. Beyond St. Pancras, half of Kings Cross Station, the neighbouring gateway to the north, can be seen. Because its style is functional it looks more modern yet is the senior by 20 years. Its clock, just distinguishable midway down the 300-ft. clock-tower of St. Pancras, came from the Crystal Palace after the 1851 Great Exhibition in Hyde Park.

Railways

For third class passengers to Glasgow from platform 6 at Euston in 1908, a rug or pillow could be hired for sixpence and left in the compartment. Unlike platform refreshments, the pillow service ended with the introduction of third class sleepers in 1928. The station master in his frock coat and top hat is at Waterloo, supervising the Ascot cups on their way to Ascot with a police escort. Beneath, the prototypes on which the present British Rail uniforms are based compared with that of the Euston guard, consulting the turnip watch kept in a leather pouch on his bandolier.

Railways (continued)

The South Eastern and Chatham railway terminus at Charing Cross, shortly after it had acquired a new flat roof to replace the one that fell into the Playhouse Theatre in 1905. Below it, a Western Blue Pullman at Paddington.

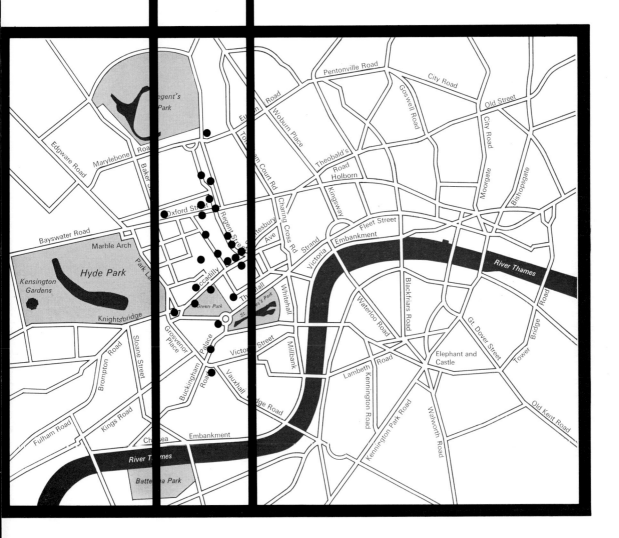

5

In the shopping streets, the window dressing and store
fronts change to meet the changing fashions but the
buildings above, to which few raise their eyes, go on
unaltered

Regent Street

On the last pages, the 18th century Quadrant that John Nash built has already been smashed apart by the huge Piccadilly Hotel, completed in 1908. It was the beginning of a programme of rebuilding that was to last until the King and Queen rode in solemn procession down a new Regent Street in 1927. The rest of the Quadrant was rebuilt to the new height, and carried over Air Street, but the heavy columns of the Piccadilly Hotel were so disliked that they were left out of the design for the rest. The Regency Quadrant had retained its elegance but the block between Conduit Street and Maddox Street, on this page, shows how Nash's original conception had deteriorated. He had designed each block of shops and businesses to look like a single building (a concept copied in the eight-storey versions of today) but the different standards of decoration, and the accretions of years to the roofline, leave the classical original indistinguishable.

This is not an earlier situation of Liberty's, closer to Piccadilly, for the store has always been at East India House, on the corner with Great Marlborough Street, from its start in 1875. This is Chesham House, opened in 1882 when the highly successful business could not find room to expand. The business was carried on in the two stores for another 40 years until the old problem was solved by the bridge across Kingly Street to the building in the Tudor style put up in 1924. Then Chesham House, so called after the birthplace of Arthur Liberty in Buckinghamshire, was given up to Lawleys.

Oxford Circus (previous page) The curved corner buildings that turn the crossing of Oxford Street by Regent Street into a circus seem of the same character at first glance but a closer look shows the contrast between the early nineteenth century Regent Street of John Nash and its twentieth century successor. The block that housed Madame Louise was rebuilt in 1911, but that on the right is in the earlier style, a comparison that Londoners were able to make over ten years for that was how long it was before any of the other three corner blocks of what was then called Regent Circus was rebuilt. Two storeys higher than any neighbour, Madame Louise towered in isolation.

Regent Street Polytechnic

The 'Poly' dates back to 1838 when a centre for lectures and exhibition was built on the corner of Cavendish Place. The famous ghost illusions of Professor Pepper, and a diving bell operating in a 5,000 gallon tank, were among the sights to be seen. It was burnt out in 1881 and Quintin Hogg, a merchant and later the first, and probably the last Lord Hailsham (for his son disclaimed the title at the first opportunity) bought it and established the 'Poly'. Rebuilding in 1911 cost £90,000. Cheap Poly travel was an early feature. The posters advertising tours of Paris, and weeks in Bonnie Scotland, outside the temporary premises, have their counterpart in the Lunn-Poly office there today.

Langham Place

Time, traffic, and German bombs
have swept away more than the
statue of Quintin Hogg, founder
of the Poly (he is safe, out of the
way of traffic, round the corner).
Beyond him, in the old photograph
on the left, is St. George's Hall,
once *the birthplace of all famous
illusions, the cemetary of superstition
and imposture* when Maskelyne and
Devant made it *England's Home of
Mystery*. Between it, and All Souls
Church, was Queens Hall, beloved
of concert-goers, 3,000 of whom
could listen at once. Both have
gone, the foreign circulating library
and palmist teashop too. The past
is remembered in the names of the
new hotel (St. Georges) and office

block (Henry Wood House, after the founder of the Promenade Concerts). Nash's 1825 place of worship, with its circular tower and ionic columns almost separated from the body of the church, ended the war with its spire shorn, and interior burned out, but restoration has spared it. Behind, in the new photograph, an extension to the BBC's Portland Place headquarters juts out.

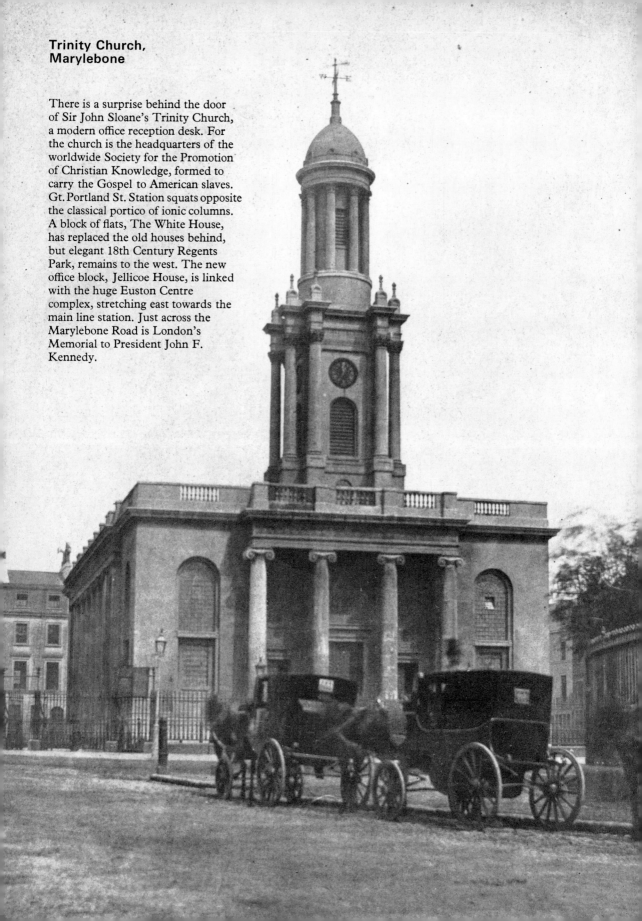

Trinity Church, Marylebone

There is a surprise behind the door of Sir John Sloane's Trinity Church, a modern office reception desk. For the church is the headquarters of the worldwide Society for the Promotion of Christian Knowledge, formed to carry the Gospel to American slaves. Gt. Portland St. Station squats opposite the classical portico of ionic columns. A block of flats, The White House, has replaced the old houses behind, but elegant 18th Century Regents Park, remains to the west. The new office block, Jellicoe House, is linked with the huge Euston Centre complex, stretching east towards the main line station. Just across the Marylebone Road is London's Memorial to President John F. Kennedy.

Oxford Street,
The John Lewis Store

Successful store owners become
desperate for extra room to expand
their businesses and John Lewis
went further than most. He went
to prison. Lewis was a buyer for
Peter Robinson before he set up
his own shop at the corner with
Holles Street in 1864. He extended
into properties to the west, as the
photograph shows, and he also
extended behind, along Holles
Street as far as Cavendish Square,
at the turn of the century. It was
here that he ran into trouble, for
he converted two corner houses,
and the ground landlord, Lord
Howard de Walden, objected to
the intrusion of commerce into the
square. He obtained a court order,
requiring Lewis to reconvert the
properties into houses. Lewis sat it
out, and eventually spent time in
gaol for his refusal to heed the
order. During the dispute he kept
London entertained by accounts
of his side of it, posted in the corner
window, under the Y of COMPANY.
There may have been one when the
photograph was taken. By amalgam-
ating with T. J. Harries and Co.,
who occupied most of the Oxford
Street buildings shown to the east,
as far as Princes Street, the John
Lewis store secured all the room it
needed for expansion after the First
World War. The mammoth store
of today, on the original site, came
after the Second World War.

ford Street, Selfridges

e original block, with flags eady flying, looks a small part the Selfridges of today, yet at e opening in 1909 it was the gest purpose-built retail store Britain. It was also described as one of the great show sights of London, for Gordon Selfridge, the American who learnt his trade with Marshall Field in Chicago, revolutionised retailing. He was the first to decorate his windows, instead of cramming them with goods. He was the first to leave the lights on until midnight. He invented the 'Bargain Basement'. Instead of intimidating his clients with gentility, he met their need for entertainment, as well as for dry goods. At first his neighbours prospered too, from the extra crowds attracted to Oxford Street, but by 1914 the long-established firm of Thomas Lloyds and Co., whose blinds turn the corner into Orchard Street, had succumbed. More of the familiar Selfridge frontage, with its stone columns reaching to the fourth floor, was built on this corner in 1923, and by 1928 a new centre portion, containing the main entrance, had been completed.

Oxford Street Woolworths

The store looks new but it is the same building that the company's own construction department built for it in 1924. Modernisation in 1962 included a new front. From this, and further development of the first floor in 1966, the selling space has become $2\frac{1}{2}$ times greater than originally. There is still a weighing machine, but inside the swinging doors.

New Bond Street

Like the Ritz, the Westbury Hot
(at the junction with Conduit
Street) has a colonnade over the
footway to allow of road widening
at small cost to the size of the hote
There are shops at ground floor
level and a main entrance round
the corner. Buildings on all four
corners of this cross-roads are new
for Bond Street suffered tremendo
damage from bombing. That
beyond the Westbury is an office
block housing, amongst others, Ai
Canada.

Old Bond Street

The *High Street of Mayfair* narrows where the delicate iron pillars front Messrs. Asprey's shop. In rooms above it, as a blue plaque records, Sir Henry Irving, the actor, lived from 1872 to 1899. In the distance is the tower of Messrs. Atkinson's, the perfumers, in which a carillon of bells was installed on its completion in 1926, a peal thought pretty by its owners. Neighbours thought otherwise and petitioned against the noise.

No low-level change beneath them
can now surprise the stone figures
of Art and Commerce as they watch
the shops re-modelled time and
again to meet the passing need or
fashion. The restlessness is not new,
for there are as many agents' notices
in the old photograph as in the new.
Even the agents change; the names
are not the same. Only Fenwick's,
down the road on the Brook Street
corner, is constant. There the store
has been since 1891 when John
James Fenwick, against all advice,
moved his successful Newcastle
business to London and beat the
local merchants on their own ground.

Berkeley Square

Commerce, entrenched on the east and south, made its first massive invasion of the west of Berkeley Square with Berger House, built in 1951-52 for the paint makers, and others, including J. Walter Thompson, the largest advertising agency in the world. Elsewhere between this and Charles Street, on the south west corner, old houses remain. But on the other side of the square, old houses survive only in the side streets, overshadowed by the towering new buildings. First on the left in Bruton Street is now Culpeper House, home of the Society of Herbalists.

The workshop of the job-masters is gone but the new structure slots in unobtrusively. The sugar-candy columns above the entrance to the newsagent have chic window boxes beside them now. Fashionable Mayfair did not use to extend this far south, yet Shepherd's Market was the heart of the May Fair, suppressed for riotousness a hundred years before the family stood soberly in their hats for their portrait, and the Daily Chronicle borrowed the billboard of the Globe. Now expensive cars from the showrooms of Piccadilly pack the narrow street between the smart shops, the flats and the eating places.

The Egyptian Hall

Built almost opposite Bond Street
as a museum of natural history,
the Egyptian Hall quickly found
live exhibits more rewarding than
dead. Some are legendary; the
original Siamese twins, and General
Tom Thumb from America, whom
12,000 people came to see. It was
John Neville Maskelyne who attached
the label *England's Home of Mystery*
to wherever he was performing,
here or at the St. George's Hall.
After providing not far short of 100
years of entertainment, especially
to the young, the Egyptian Hall was
demolished in 1905 and a block of
shops and offices, sentimentally
called Egyptian House was erected
in its place.

Piccadilly

The artists cherished by the Royal Institute of Painters in Water Colour look out from their galleries, but not down at the intrusive airline sign. Beneath the galleries, where the Royal Society of Oil Painters exhibits too, much is changed. The Princes Restaurant, photographed here a dozen years after the building was put up in 1883, passed away between the wars. Many of the smart shops of Piccadilly were rebuilt in the 'twenties. Meakers, on the right opposite, in 1926 and Fortnum and Mason, on the other side of the road, in the following year. The arts have another home in Burlington House, also on the right shown fully in the new photograph Burlington Arcade, the entrance to which is furthest left in the new photograph, dates back to 1819.

There were bicycles, horsebuses and hansom cabs for ordinary people but the wealthy had motorcars already when the luxurious Ritz Hotel, its colonnade extending over the footway, was opened in 1906. It was the first London building to be steel-framed but the advance was felt to be, like plumbing, something to disguise. Green Park has been in retreat since. The Underground station was built in 1933 but today's blockhouses are related to the new Victoria Line, opened early in 1969.

Piccadilly (the clubs)

Always anonymous, the clubs diminish imperceptibly; only the St. James's, shrinking between its neighbours, survives in this view. It was opened for diplomats in 1858 in a mid-eighteenth century house. To the left, the Park Lane Hotel, fifteen years in the building and completed in 1927, expanded later to swallow the Saville Club, in the house with the bow corner, once the home of Nathan Rothschild, who made a great fortune by being first to know the result of Waterloo. Right of the St. James's, the elegant house of 1870 has been several times an hotel and once a club, the Ishmian. Three storeys were added to the roof in 1927 to increase accommodation. Profligate living so ruined its eighteenth century owner that he had to dress bailiffs as footmen whenever inviting guests to dinner. Now the Arts Council of Great Britain has the ground floor. Beyond it, the massive premises of the old Junior Constitutional Club are to let. The park has retreated and the road is wider.

St James's Palace

Patrolling sentries from the Brigade of Guards are reminders that the Court was here for the 140 years between the burning of Whitehall Palace and the accession of Queen Victoria. St. James's Palace had been the home of kings for much longer. Henry VIII built it and the gatehouse and clocktower survive from his palace. The doors, in linen-fold panelling, are original too. The name comes from an earlier building with a much different purpose. It was a leper hospital, dedicated to St. James the Less, for the support of which a May Fair was held each year, an event which gave the district its name.

Duke of Wellington Place

Scorning the honeycomb of subways and underpass, the Duke on horseback waits on for a break in the traffic, opposite Apsley House, the home with the best address, No. 1 London. A new junction with Park Lane now divides the islanded but little-changed Wellington museum from its neighbours, perhaps a proper separation for the imperfect but much-loved Lady Hamilton lived on the other side. Old Park Lane winds into Piccadilly further up, beyond Hamilton Place which lies opposite the underpass entrance and is named after a Hyde Park ranger, not Emma. The new exit and bomb damage has left the terraced mansions gap-toothed. The ordinary motor-van of old has evolved into a vehicle uniquely adapted to the transport, storage and sale of ice cream.

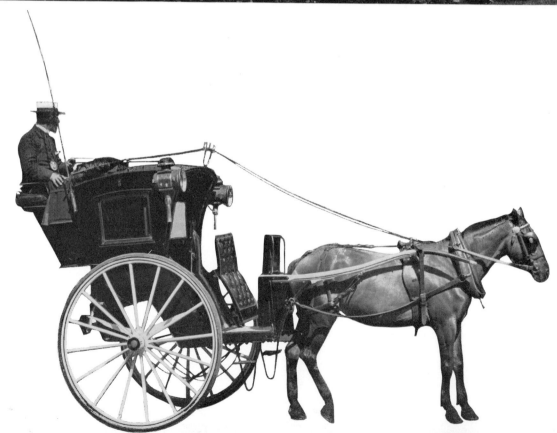

Buckingham Palace

To make it fit for a King the palace built on the site of the mansion that King George III had bought from John Sheffield, Duke of Buckingham, was re-fronted in 1912, eight years after the white marble memorial to Queen Victoria was put up outside. The new Portland Stone front cost £60,000, but was built in only three months, while the Royal Family was away for the summer. So pleased was King George V on his return that he invited all the workmen in to dinner. Once Marble Arch, now at a corner of Hyde Park, stood in the forecourt of palace.

Victoria Station

Once rare, motor-buses now crowd
to the doors of Victoria Station, first
of the great southern rail termini to
be built north of the Thames, and
the courtyard has given way to their
stands. Once the tiny Victoria
Station and Pimlico Railway owned
the building, leasing the lines to the
big South Eastern and Chatham
Railway, the Great Western Railway,

and the Brighton and South Coast
Railway (see the name faintly over
the stations it served). Re-building
in the first years of the century cost
£2 million. For today's Southern
Region of British Rail, it remains the
Gateway to the Continent. The sea
passage, still an hour away from
Dover, has itself been halved by the
hovercraft.

171

London Fire Brigade

The first motor-driven fire engines came in after the old Metropolitan Fire Brigade changed its name in 1904. The brigade had taken over in 1866 from the old insurance offices who had banded together to protect their premium income with horse-drawn engines. Ten years later the brigade numbered 80 men and today it numbers 5,500 men, having grown with London to protect all the 52 boroughs in the 620 square miles of the Greater London Council area. From 120 stations, it handles 5 million feet of hose and has 550 appliances which includes only two fireboats. Firebrace is one, standing out from its pier close to the Lambeth brigade headquarters to practise opposite the Houses of Parliament, successor to Beta, which cost the old LCC £10,000 in 1906. The brigade is called out 60,000 times a year, though not all the calls are to fires. In a recent year they included 22 people stuck in railings, 115 animal rescues and 1,180 cases of people trapped in lifts.

Buckingham Palace Road

On the right, beneath the shades, is the store that Frederick Gorringe opened in 1858, called the "village shop of Buckingham Palace", for the ladies-in-waiting would step across to make their small purchases, certain that no intrusive assistant would be so forward as to say, "It is nice, isn't it, Madam" or "The colour suits you" for they were forbidden to say a word until first addressed. On the left, behind the glass, is the great modern store into which the business transferred, but it was not a success, and moved away, leaving the windows empty.

6

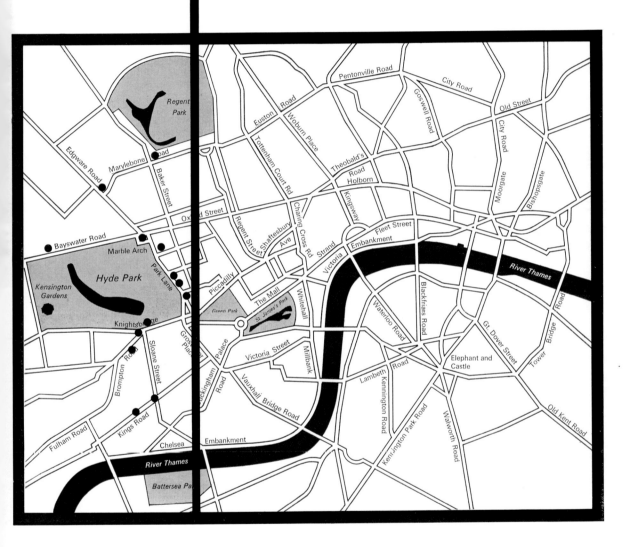

From the wealth of Park Lane, the camera follows the
three sides of Hyde Park to end in the London of today,
in Chelsea

Park Lane

Once a by-word for the London wealthy, Park Lane is now the home of a Hilton Hotel, the by-word for American affluence in the capitals of the world. It was completed in 1963 and rises to 24 storeys. The poets fountain, with figures of Chaucer, Shakespeare and Milton, surmounted by fame blowing its trumpet, was the whim of an old lady who died without heirs. It cost £5,000 in 1875 and the money came from her estate. The figures were battered by bombs but stayed on mutilated until 1949. Rivers of traffic, divided into half a dozen and more streams, now separate Park Lane from Hyde Park.

No. 93 Park Lane, or as it was then called, No. 1 Grosvenor Gate (because of the entrance to Hyde Park opposite) was the home of Benjamin Disraeli from 1839 to 1872, as the plaque on the wall behind the traffic signal recalls. These smaller, bow-fronted houses, dating back to the middle of the 18th century, saw the great Victorian palaces of Park Lane come and go, replaced by the hotels and blocks of flats and offices of today. They have long fallen out of private use. Most are offices, but the tallest, in the darkest brick, is the Embassy of the People's Republic of South Yemen.

Why is Dorchester House, described at the time as *the finest residence in London*, flying the Stars and Stripes? Because it is let to the American Ambassador, Mr. Whitelaw Reid, and it is at his invitation that the horse- and motor-carriages are bringing society to its doors. There is an American eagle in the garden, too. Dorchester House was built in the style of an Italian palace by Villiamy for the Holford family in 1851. Its marble staircase alone was said to have cost £30,000. It was often let, even in the last century, and foreign potentates who made it their home included the Shah of Persia. Later, nobody could be found to take the lease and the house stood empty for a number of years before it was demolished in 1929. The tradition of luxury was continued by the 400 room Dorchester Hotel, built for £1¾ million in 1931.

9160. MARBLE ARCH.

Marble Arch

Photographed from Edgware Road, the motor cars and buses look well-spaced newcomers but the first major road change to accommodate them had already been made. In 1902 the park railings were set back to let road traffic pass behind the arch, leaving it a traffic island instead of a gateway into Hyde Park. In 1960 the Park retreated further, when its East Carriage Road became a second track for Park Lane, and the traffic complex became so large that there is again space to stroll about behind the arch, as they did in the last century (overleaf) except that the stroller must go underground to reach it, and to find the spot where the gallows stood when this was Tyburn, the place of execution. Marble Arch was built by John Nash in front of Buckingham Palace in 1828 and had on its top the bronze statue of King George IV which now stands in a corner of Trafalgar Square.

Grosvenor Square

The first American Minister to the Court of St. James, John Adams, lived in Grosvenor Square, So did Lord North, the Prime Minister whose high-handedness cost Britain her American colonies. Twenty-five years ago the west side was eight buildings, and the American Embassy was across the road at Number One, now the home of the Canadian High Commission. Now the 1960 embassy takes up the whole of the west side, its nine floors extending half as far below ground as above. Only the lamp standard identifies the camera's viewpoint and this survival is interesting for Grosvenor Square, long the home of the noble and influential, was the last important place in London to install gas lighting in 1842, one hundred years before the earlier photograph was taken.

Marks and Spencer, Edgware Road

The Edgware Road Penny Bazaar opened in time for the Christmas of 1912. It had a new front in 1920, and another in 1928 when the shop next door was taken in. It expanded upstairs, as well as sideways but after the block was re-developed in 1959, Marks and Spencer became tenants of 20,000 square feet of selling area on two floors of the new building, giving them five times more space than their first shop.

Marylebone Road

The hoarding read *Travel from this station to the British Empire Exhibition in Wembley Park*. The year was 1924, the return fare from Baker Street Underground station was 1s and 650 trains a day were making the ten minute journey, for this was the quickest route from the centre. In the following year, the station forecourt was lit by the glare of a great fire as Madame Tussaud's waxworks was burned down on its other side. Marylebone Road was ready for change. The Metropolitan Railway Co. built Chiltern Court, the block of flats and shops, over the station in 1927 and Arnold Bennett was an early

tenant. He died there in 1931. Next to it, Berkeley Court, was built later and dominates the modern photograph. Marylebone Road was always wide because the long gardens which led to it from the first houses were taken in at the start of the motor age. Beneath it, the first underground passenger railway ran from 1863, a fact recorded on the station wall, a corner of which is all that remains of the old in the new on the right of the photographs. On the left in both, however, is glimpsed the massive Bickenhall mansions, built in 1897, the first block of flats of all in Marylebone Road.

Bayswater Road

Only the trees become grander.
Half the block of solid houses east
of Hyde Park Street is gone, replaced by new flats, half remains
but is converted into flats. Rosehill
Lodge is sold and empty, rubbing
shoulders with commerce and wait-
ing for the end. Porchester Gardens
has become flats, too, and hides its
arched windows behind the thriving
trees.

m the Hyde Park Hotel look
t or east and all the buildings
e erected a few years either side
he beginning of this century.
e big stores, Woollands, loom-
largest on this page; Harvey
hols, on the left of the opposite
e; the massive block between
ightsbridge and the Brompton
ad, with the Scotch House at
tip; the red brick and white
ne striped block in the opposite
ection, the last before Hyde Park
ner; and the Hyde Park Hotel
elf. All except the French Em-
ssy, its ground floor blocked by
e open-topped omnibus, and its
npanion mansion on the opposite
e of Albert Gate, which were
ilt speculatively fifty years earlier,
od empty and were nicknamed
alta and Gibraltar because they
re *too large to be taken*. Only
water House, out of sight where
e covered ways ran down to the
vement from the houses it re-
aced, is of this half of the century.
t change lies in the future for
e Woollands store is closed and
uttered and is to be demolished
d replaced by a new hotel.

Sloane Square

A road ran across the middle of the square until the coming of motor cars when the centre was paved, trees planted and traffic made to go round. Peter Jones, firs established in Draycott Avenue in 1871, transferred to Kings Road and stretched along it, the biggest draper in Chelsea, but not reaching Sloane Square until the public house and row of houses which formed the west side were bought after the Great War. The new store was built between 1936 and 1939 and was the first curtain wall building in Britain. The buildings on the south side are unchanged, and go back to 1891.

Harrods Knightsbridge

Henry Charles Harrod, a tea merchant, was nearly 50 when he took over a grocery shop belonging to a friend in 1849. His son, Charles Digby, took control of it 12 years later. Behind the great expansion before and after the store became a limited liability company in 1889 was its first general manager, Richard Burbidge. A former manager of Whiteley's provision department, his working day began with breakfast at the store at 7 a.m. Development of the site, which eventually totalled $4\frac{1}{2}$ acres, was continuous but the terra-cotta Brompton Road frontage dated from 1902, about the time the telegraphic address *Everything, London* was adopted.

Kings Road, Chelsea

Although not a directly contrasted
viewpoint, no better contrast could
there be between the Kings Road
of old, unknown to fashion, and
that of today. Where once worthy
shopkeepers provided the means to
support life, now the boutiques sell
the ephemera of life. The scene is
no longer indigenous but inter-
national; the Drugstore here pictured
borrows its name from America
and copies its shape from a Paris
counterpart.